THE WONDERFUL DRAMA OF PUNCH AND JUDY

"THE WONDERFUL DRAMA OF PUNCH AND JUDY

BY PAPERNOSE WOODENSCONCE ESQ

WITH ILLUSTRATIONS BY "THE OWL."

LONDON:
JAMES BLACKWOOD, PATERNOSTER ROW.

PUNCH AND JUDY, BABBY, AND THEIR LITTLE DOG TOBY.

THE WONDERFUL DRAMA

PUNCH AND JUDY

AND THEIR

LITTLE DOG TOBY,

AS PERFORMED TO

OVERFLOWING BALCONIES AT THE CORNER OF THE STREET.

—◁≪●≫▷—

CORRECTED AND REVISED,
FROM THE ORIGINAL MANUSCRIPT IN THE POSSESSION OF THE KING OF THE CANNIBAL ISLANDS,
BY PERMISSION OF HIS MAJESTY'S LIBRARIAN ;

WITH NOTES AND REFERENCES.

BY PAPERNOSE WOODENSCONCE, ESQ.

———

With Illustrations by " The Owl."

———

LONDON:
JAMES BLACKWOOD, PATERNOSTER ROW.

ISBN 978-1-4341-0562-2

Published by Waking Lion Press, an imprint of the Editorium

Waking Lion Press™ and Editorium™ are trademarks of:

The Editorium, LLC
West Jordan, UT 84081-6132
www.editorium.com

PREFACE.

THE want of a good acting edition of *Punch and Judy* has long been felt, chiefly by ambitious young gentlemen aspiring to give private representations of that world-famous drama. The present volume is designed to supply the important deficiency; and the Editor can assert with confidence, that no pains have been spared to render it a complete work. The original text, carefully pruned of all excrescences, has been rigidly adhered to. The Ghost, too often omitted by syco-phantic Showmen in deference to the squeamishness of the age, has been preserved, and the two Fighting-Men discarded, as a weak-minded innovation. The Foreigner, unwarrantably supplanted by the Jim Crow of our own day (who has notoriously no business in the piece at all), has been restored to his original position. The most striking scenes have been illustrated by a skilful artist. Foot-notes have been appended wherever necessary; and verses, in elucidation of the high moral purpose of the drama, appended to each scene.

By a careful study of the dialogue and stage-directions, coupled with a diligent and frequent rehearsal of the squeak (which is not difficult, and may be practised at the top of the house), a youth of average abilities may, in a comparatively short time, acquire such a proficiency in the art of performing Punch, as to render an apprenticeship to a regular professor (to which most parents, on its proposal, would be found to object) wholly unnecessary.

PAPERNOSE WOODENSCONCE.

Short's Buildings, St. Giles's.

Persons represented.

MR. PUNCH, *the father of a family.*

TOBY, *his dog.*

JOEY, *a clown, his friend.*

THE BEADLE, *an officer, his enemy.*

A DISTINGUISHED FOREIGNER, *imperfectly acquainted with the English language.*

JONES, *a respectable tradesman.*

THE HANGMAN, *ditto.*

A DOCTOR (*of physic*).

███████████████████ *a horrid, dreadful personage.*

JUDY, *Punch's wife, the mother of a family.*

A BABY, *the family aforesaid.*

A GHO-O-O-O-O-OST ! ! ! ! ! !

The Voice of the spirited Proprietor, supposed to be in the street below, minding his drum and looking after the coppers.

SCENE I.—PROLOGUE.

Music. *The spirited Proprietor plays " Pop goes the weasel," or any other popular melody, as much out of tune as possible.* *Curtain rises.*

Punch (below). Root to-to-to-to-too-o-o-it!

Proprietor. Now, Mister Punch, I 'ope you're ready

Punch. Shan't be a minute; I'm only putting on my boots.

Prop. (perfectly satisfied with the explanation.) Werry good, sir.

[*He plays with increased vigour.*

Punch (pops up.) Root-to-to-to-to-it!

Prop. Well, Mister Punch, 'ow de do?

Punch. How de do?

Prop. (affably). I am pooty well, Mister Punch, I thank you.

Punch. Play us up a bit of a dance.

Prop. Cert'ny, Mister Punch.   [*Music.   Punch dances.*

Punch. Stop!   Did you ever see my wife?

Prop. (with dignity). I never know'd as 'ow you was married, Mister Punch.

Punch. Oh! I've got such a splendid wife! (*Calling below.*) Judy!—Judy, my darling!—Judy, my duck of several diamonds!

MR. PUNCH.

Behold the bloated form of Punch!
 His reddened nose, with pimples on;
His stomach vast, and shapeless hunch,
 Resembling much your Uncle John!
Avoid excess at dinner or at lunch,
Unless you'd look like Uncle John or Punch.

Scene II.—Punch and Judy.

Punch (admiring his Wife). Ain't she a beauty? There's a nose! Give us a kiss. (*They embrace fondly.*) Now play up.

> [*They dance. At the conclusion, Punch hits his Wife on the head with his stick.*

Prop. (severely). Mister Punch, that's very wrong.

Punch. Haven't I a right to do what I like with my own?

Judy (taking stick from him). In course he has. (*Hitting Punch.*) Take that!

Punch. Oh!

Judy (hitting him again). Oh!

Punch. Oh!

Judy (hitting him again). Oh!

Punch (taking stick frm her, and knocking her out of sight). Oh! That was to request her to step downstairs to dress the babby. Such a beautiful babby, you've no idea. I'll go and fetch him.

PUNCH HAS A LITTLE MISUNDERSTANDING WITH HIS WIFE.

Punch with a stick his wife attacks,
   The wife to whom he vowed to cling,—
Joined by the force of love, not whacks:
   A most improper sort of thing!
My little readers, as you love your lives,
I trust that none of you ill-treat your wives!

SCENE III.—PUNCH RISES WITH HIS INFANT SON IN HIS ARMS.

Punch (*sings*).   " Hush-a-bye, baby,
And sleep while you can;
If you live till you're older,
You'll grow up a man."

Did you ever see such a beautiful child? and so good?

The Child (*cries*). Mam-ma-a-a!

Punch (*thumping him with stick*). Go to sleep, you brat! (*Resumes his song.*)

" Hush-a-bye, baby,"—

The Child (*louder*). Mam-ma-a-a-a!

Punch (*hitting harder*).   Go to sleep!

The Child (*yells*). Ya-a-a-ah-ah!

Punch (*hitting him*). Be quiet! Bless him, he's got his father's nose! (*The Child seizes Punch by the nose.*)   Murder! Let go!   There, go to your mother, if you can't be good.

Throws Child out of window.

PUNCH THROWS HIS SON OUT OF WINDOW.

The baby squalls, the baby kicks,
    As babies we have often seen do;
But still, to beat them so with sticks,
    And then to throw them out of window,
Is not the way to make them better grow:
Besides, it might hurt somebody below.

Scene IV.—The untimely End of Judy.

Punch (sings, *drumming with his legs on the front of the stage*).

"She's all my fancy painted her,
She's lovely, she's divine!"

Enter Judy (*with maternal anxiety depicted on her countenance*).

Judy. Where's the boy?

Punch. The boy?

Judy. Yes.

Punch. What! didn't you catch him?

Judy. Catch him?

Punch. Yes; I threw him out of window. I thought you might be passing.

Judy. Oh! my poor child! Oh! my poor child!

Punch. Why, he was as much mine as yours.

Judy. But you shall pay for it; I'll tear your eyes out.

Punch. Root-to-to-to-to-oo-it!   [*Kills her at a blow.*

Prop. Mr. Punch, you 'ave committed a barbarous and cruel murder, and you must hanswer for it to the laws of your country.

THE BARBAROUS MURDER OF JUDY.

Punch worse and worse we see has grown,
    And seems at human law to scoff;
His child he's out of window thrown,
    And now his wife has finish'd off.
He's a sad scamp!   You wish to know where he
Expects to go to?—stop a bit—we'll see.

Scene V.—Punch is arrested by the Beadle.

The Beadle (entering brandishing his staff of office). Holloa! holloa! holloa! here I am!

Punch. Holloa! holloa! holloa! and so am I!   [*Hits Beadle.*

Beadle. Do you see my staff, sir?

Punch. Do you feel mine?   [*Hits him again.*

Beadle (beating time with his truncheon). I am the Beadle, Churchwarden, Overseer, Street-keeper, Turncock, Stipendiary Magistrate, and Beadle of the parish!

Punch. Oh! you are the Beagle, Church-warming-pan, Street-sweeper, Turniptop, Stupendiary Magistrate, and Black-beetle of the parish?

Beadle. I am the Beadle.

Punch. And so am I.

Beadle. You a Beadle?

Punch. Yes.

Beadle. Where's your authority?

Punch. There it is!   [*Knocks him down.*

PUNCH IS ARRESTED BY THE BEADLE.

The Beadle comes, a man of law,
    Armed with the most tremendous powers;
Like him whose scoldings you've, with awe,
    Caught in the square, for picking flowers.
In such a case I hope (have you such failings?)
You don't make faces at him through the railings.

SCENE VI.—PUNCH AND THE BEADLE (*continued*).

Beadle (*rising*). Mr. Punch, you are an ugly, ill-bred fellow.

Punch. And so are you.

Beadle. Take your nose out of my face, sir.

Punch. Take your face out of my nose, sir.

Beadle. Pooh!

Punch. Pooh!   [*Hits him.*

Beadle (*appealing to the Proprietor*). Young man, you are a witness that he has committed an aggravated assault on the majesty of the law.

Punch. Oh! he'd swear anything.

Prop. (*in a reconciling tone*). Don't take no notice of what he says.

Punch. For he'd swear through a brick.

Beadle. It's a conspiracy; I can see through it.

Prop. Through what?

Punch. Through a brick.

Beadle. This mustn't go on, Mr. Punch; I am under the necessity of taking you up.

Punch. And I am under the necessity of knocking you down.

         [*The Beadle falls a lifeless corpse.*

Punch (*in ecstasies*). Roo-to-to-to-to-it!

PUNCH KILLS THE BEADLE.

At it again! to do what's right,
    Punch nothing can compel or wheedle.
Would you believe it? in his spite
    He's been and gone and killed the Beadle!
I view the horrid crime with consternation:
Beadles are mortals; that's some consolation.

Scene VII.

Enter a Distinguished Foreigner,* *popping up under* Punch's *nose.*

The Distinguished Foreigner. Shallabala !

        [*Punch aims at and misses him. He disap-*
            pears and bobs up on the other side.

The Illustrious Stranger. Shallabala !

        [*Punch makes another failure. The Interesting*
            Alien bobs up in another direction.

The Native of other Lands. Shallabala !

Punch Why don't you speak English ?

The Continental Personage. Because I can't.

Punch. Oh ! [*He lays the Man from Abroad dead at one blow.*

The Expiring Immigrant. Shallabala !   [*He dies.*

Punch (exultingly).   Root-to-to-to-to-it !

       * Supposed to be the Hospodar of Wallachia.

PUNCH RECEIVES A FOREIGN VISITOR WITH OLD-ENGLISH HOSPITALITY.

Behold the Foreigner, unshorn,
    As hairy as a bear or rabbit:
Think how your grandmammas would mourn,
    If you indulged in such a habit.
Be warned, all boys upon this picture gazers—
    Shave twice a week at least, and keep good razors!

SCENE VIII. (IN DUMB SHOW).—PUNCH AND THE GHO-O-O-OST!!!*

Punch exults over his successful crimes in a heartless manner, by singing a fragment of a popular melody, and drumming with his heels upon the front of the stage.

Mysterious music, announcing the appearance of the Gho-o-o-o-ost!!! who rises and places its unearthly hands upon the bodies of Punch's victims in an awful and imposing manner. The bodies rise slowly.

* We have been at great pains to find out of whom this fearful apparition is supposed to be the departed spirit. The result of our labours has been, that we haven't.

THE GHO-O-O-O-O-OST ! ! ! ! ! !

This is a Ghost! Some folks declare
    That in the world there's never been one.
Now, story-telling's wrong; take care
    None of you say you've never seen one—
Having been shown the one these lines o'ertopping—
That is, unless you want to catch a whopping.

Scene IX.—Punch and the Gho-o-o-o-ost!!! (*continued*)

Punch (*in the same hardened manner, as yet unconscious of the approaching terrors*).

> " Rum ti tum ti iddity um.
>   Pop goes "——

The Ghost. Boo-o-o-o-oh!

Punch (*frightened*). A-a-a-a-ah!

    [*He kicks frantically, and is supposed to turn deadly pale.*

Ghost. Boo-o-o-o-oh!

Punch. A-a-a-a-ah!   [*He trembles like a leaf.*

Ghost. Boo-o-o-o-oh!!!

       [*Punch faints. The Ghost and bodies disappear. Punch, by spasmodic convulsions, expresses that the terrors of a guilty conscience, added to the excesses of an irregular course of life, have brought on an intermittent fever.*

Punch (*feebly*). I'm very ill: fetch a Doctor. [*Doctor rises.*

Doctor. Somebody called for a Doctor. Why, I declare it's my old friend Punch. What's the matter with him?

PUNCH IS FRIGHTENED.

You've heard of people looking blue,—
　　Punch, whom you've seen as red as poppy,
You now perceive of violet hue—
　　That's if you've bought a coloured copy.
If not, you needn't with regret be stirr'd for it,—
Suppose him blue, and take the author's word for it.

SCENE X.—PUNCH ON A SICK-BED, ATTENDED BY THE DOCTOR.

The Doctor (feeling the patient's pulse). Fourteen—fifteen —nineteen—six. The man is not dead—almost, quite. Punch, *are* you dead?

Punch (starting up and hitting him). Yes.

[*He relapses into insensibility.*

Doctor. Mr. Punch, there's no believing you; I don't believe you are dead.

Punch (hitting him as before). Yes, I am.

Doctor. I tell you what, Punch, I must go and fetch you some physic. [*Exit.*

Punch (rising). A pretty Doctor, to come without physic.

Re-enter Doctor, with a cudgel. Punch relapses as before.

Doctor. Now, Punch, *are* you dead? No reply! (*Thrashing him.*) Physic! physic! physic!

[*The mixture as before is repeated each time.*

PUNCH IS ATTENDED BY HIS MEDICAL ADVISER.

Punch has behaved extremely ill:
 In fact, I fear there's no denying
He's an atrocious rascal! Still,
 When at the Doctor's mercy lying,
Shouldn't we some compassion feel—I *ask* all.
My youthful readers—even for a rascal?

SCENE XI.—PUNCH AND THE DOCTOR (*continued*).

Punch (*reviving under the influence of the dose*). What sort of physic do you call that, Doctor?

Doctor. Stick-liquorice! stick-liquorice! stick-liquorice!

      [*The mixture as before repeated each time.*

Punch. Stop, Doctor! give me the bottle in my own hands. (*Taking stick from him, and thrashing him with it.*) Physic! physic! physic! (*Doctor yells.*) What a simple Doctor! doesn't like his own physic! Stick-liquorice! stick-liquorice! stick-liquorice!

Doctor (*calling out*). Punch, pay me my fee, and let me go.

Punch. What's your fee?

Doctor. A guinea.

Punch. Give me change out of a fourpenny-bit.

Doctor. But a guinea's twenty-one shillings.

Punch. Stop! let me feel for my purse. (*Takes up stick and hits Doctor.*) One! two! three! four! Stop! that was a bad one; I'll give you another. Four! five! six!

    [*Hits Doctor twenty-one times. Then looks at*
       him. He is motionless.

Punch. Root-to-to-to-to-it! Settled!

PUNCH SETTLES HIS DOCTOR'S BILL.

Punch has received the Doctor's physic,
    And sends it back to whence it came:
Is there a little boy who *is* sick
    Who wouldn't like to do the same?
In my own case, I know, if I could find
That Doctor Camomile—but never mind!

Scene XII.—A Friend visits Punch.

Punch (sings).

> " I dreamt that I dwelt in marble halls,
>> With vassals and serfs by my side;
> And of all who assembled within those proud walls,
>> That I was the joy and the" ——

> [*Joey the Clown rises, and takes up the body of the Doctor, whose head he bobs in Punch's face.*

Joey. Bob !

Punch (rubbing his nose). Who said " bob " ?

Joey (knocking Doctor into his face again). Bob ! bob ! bob !

Punch. Bob ! bob ! bob ! (*Knocks Doctor out of sight, and sees Joey.*) Ah, Joey ! was that you ?

Joey. Yes ; how's your mother ?

Punch. Well, don't do it again.

Joey. Why not ?

Punch. Because I'm nervous ! Come and feel how my hand shakes. (*Joey approaches. Punch aims a blow at him, which he dodges.*) Come a little nearer ! I won't hurt you.

Joey (to Proprietor.) Do you think he will, Mister ?

Proprietor. Well, Joey, I shouldn't think as 'ow he would, if so be as he calls hisself a gentleman.

Joey. I'll try him.

JOEY THE CLOWN PLAYS AN UNFRIENDLY TRICK ON PUNCH.

Lives there a youth who has not yearned
 To be, at least to dress, like Clown;
And up his trouser-ankles turned,
 And of his mouth the corners down?
To do Clown well—here's a good lesson—con it !—
Whiten your face, and stick red wafers on it.

Scene XIII.—Punch and his Friend Joey (continued).

Joey, assured of the friendly intentions of Punch, approaches him. Punch aims a vigorous blow at him, which he again avoids, by dodging to the other side.

Punch. There! it didn't hurt, did it?

Joey. No.

Punch. (*aims again. Joey avoids blow as before*). Nor that?

Joey. No.

Punch (*as before*). Nor that?

Joey. Not a bit.

Punch. Then what are you afraid of? Come and shake hands.

Joey (*to Proprietor*). Do you think I'm safe, Mister?

Proprietor. Cert'ny, Joey; Mr. Punch 'as behaved hisself like a man of his word. [*Joey approaches Punch to shake hands. Punch aims at him. Joey avoids blow as before.*

Punch. Joey, you're a coward.

Joey. Don't call names.

Punch. Then fight fair.

Joey. Come on. [*Music, " Drops of Brandy." They fight, Joey avoiding all Punch's blows.*

PUNCH DISAGREES WITH HIS FRIEND,

Punch, always anxious for a quarrel,
   Gets up a skirmish with his friend;
From which I draw a splendid moral,
   To which I hope you'll all attend:
When Master Tomkins comes to spend the day,
Don't send him—say, with *two* black eyes—away!

Scene XIV.—The Fight between Punch and Joey (*continued*).

Punch (*aiming a blow at Joey on the right side of the stage*). There!

Joey (*appearing on the left*).   No! here!

Punch. Oh, very good. There!   [*Misses again.*

Joey (*popping up his head in front, under the curtains*). Where?

Punch (*aims at him*).   There!   [*Misses and looks over.*

Joey (*putting his head outside curtains, on the right*).   Mr. Punch, that was a foul blow.

Punch. Then here's a fair one.

> [*Aims again. Joey disappears. Punch looks round the curtains, watching for him.*

Joey (*putting his head out on the other side*).   Now, Mr. Punch, I'm ready.

Punch. And I'm willing.

> [*Turns quickly round and hits at him again. Joey disappears as before. Fight continues, Joey always vanishing when Punch aims a blow, and appearing in an opposite direction. At last Punch lays down his stick, and peeps cautiously round the curtains to watch for Joey.*

Punch. I've got him now!

Joey (*rising behind him, and seizing stick*).   And how do you like him?   [*Larrups Punch.*

Punch. Murder! thieves! Toby, come and help your master!

> [*Toby barks below. Joey disappears.*

PUNCH MEETS WITH HIS MATCH.

Joey the Clown, by constant dodging,
  Successfully avoids the blows
Which Punch desirous is of lodging
  On a part vital—say his nose.
Quite right! when folks of thrashing you are thinking,
Punish them soundly—that is, cut like winking!

Scene XV.—Punch and Toby.

Toby rises, barking. Punch embraces him.

Punch. There's a beautiful dog! I knew he'd come to help his master; he's so fond of me. Poor little fellow! Toby, ain't you fond of your master? [*Toby snaps.*

Punch. Oh, my nose!

Proprietor. Mr. Punch, you don't conciliate the hanimal properly; you should promise him something nice for supper.

Punch. Toby, you shall have a pail of water and a broomstick for supper. (*Toby snaps again.*) I'll knock your brains out.

Proprietor. Don't go to hurt the dog, Mr. Punch.

Punch. I will.

Proprietor. Don't!

Punch. I'll knock his brains out, and cut his throat!

Proprietor. How, with your stick?

Punch. I will! So here goes. One! two! (*Jones, a respectable tradesman, Toby's former master, rises, and receives the blow intended for Toby on his head.*) Three!

Jones. Murder!

PUNCH AND HIS WONDERFUL DOG TOBY.

Toby appears—a dog of fame !
    Perhaps you've heard historians tell
About a pig who bore the name,
    Who read and spelt extremely well.
Let this, in learning, lead to progress big ;
In scholarship, who'd be behind a pig ?

SCENE XVII.—PUNCH, TOBY, AND JONES (*a respectable Tradesman*), *continued.*

Punch (*to Jones*). We'll soon see. (*Goes up to Toby.*) "Toby, poor little fellow, how are you?" [*Toby snaps at Punch's nose.*

Jones. There! you see!

Punch. What?

Jones. That shows the dog's mine.

Punch. No; it shows he's mine.

Jones. Then if he's yours, why does he bite you?

Punch. Because he likes me.

Jones. Pooh! nonsense! we'll soon settle which of us the dog belongs to, Mr. Punch. We'll fight for him. I'll have the dog to back me up. Toby, I'm going to fight for your liberty. If Punch knocks me down, you pick me up; if Punch wollops me, you wollop him.

Punch. But I'm not going to fight three or four of you.

Jones. The dog is only going to back me up.

Punch. Then somebody must back me up. (*To Proprietor.*) Will you back me up, sir?

Prop. (*always willing to oblige.*) Cert'ny, Mr. Punch.

[*They take places for a fight.*

TOBY SHOWS HIS AFFECTION FOR PUNCH.

Toby to bite off Punch's nose
    Attempts; it's true there's plenty of it;
And Punch can well afford to lose
    A little: but I hope you'll profit
(You who have smaller noses) by the sight,—
Don't make companions of small dogs that bite.

Scene XVIII.—Punch, Toby, and Jones (*the respectable Tradesman*), *continued.*

Prop. Now, you don't begin till I say "time." (*Punch knocks Jones down*). Mr. Punch, that wasn't fair.

Punch. Why, you said time.

Prop. I didn't.

Punch. What did you say, then?

Prop. I said, " You don't begin till I say ' time.' "

Punch. There! you said it again. [*Knocks Jones down again.*

Jones. Toby, I'm down! back me up. [*Toby flies at Punch.*

Toby. G-r-r-r-r-r-r ! [*Bites Punch.*

Punch. It isn't fair ; he didn't say " time."

Jones. At him again, Toby ! Good dog !

Toby. G-r-r-r-row-wow ! [*Bites again.*

Punch. Murder ! I say, sir, please to call him off.

Prop. Mr. Punch, you must wait till I say " time."

[*Toby attacks Punch furiously, defending his former master.*

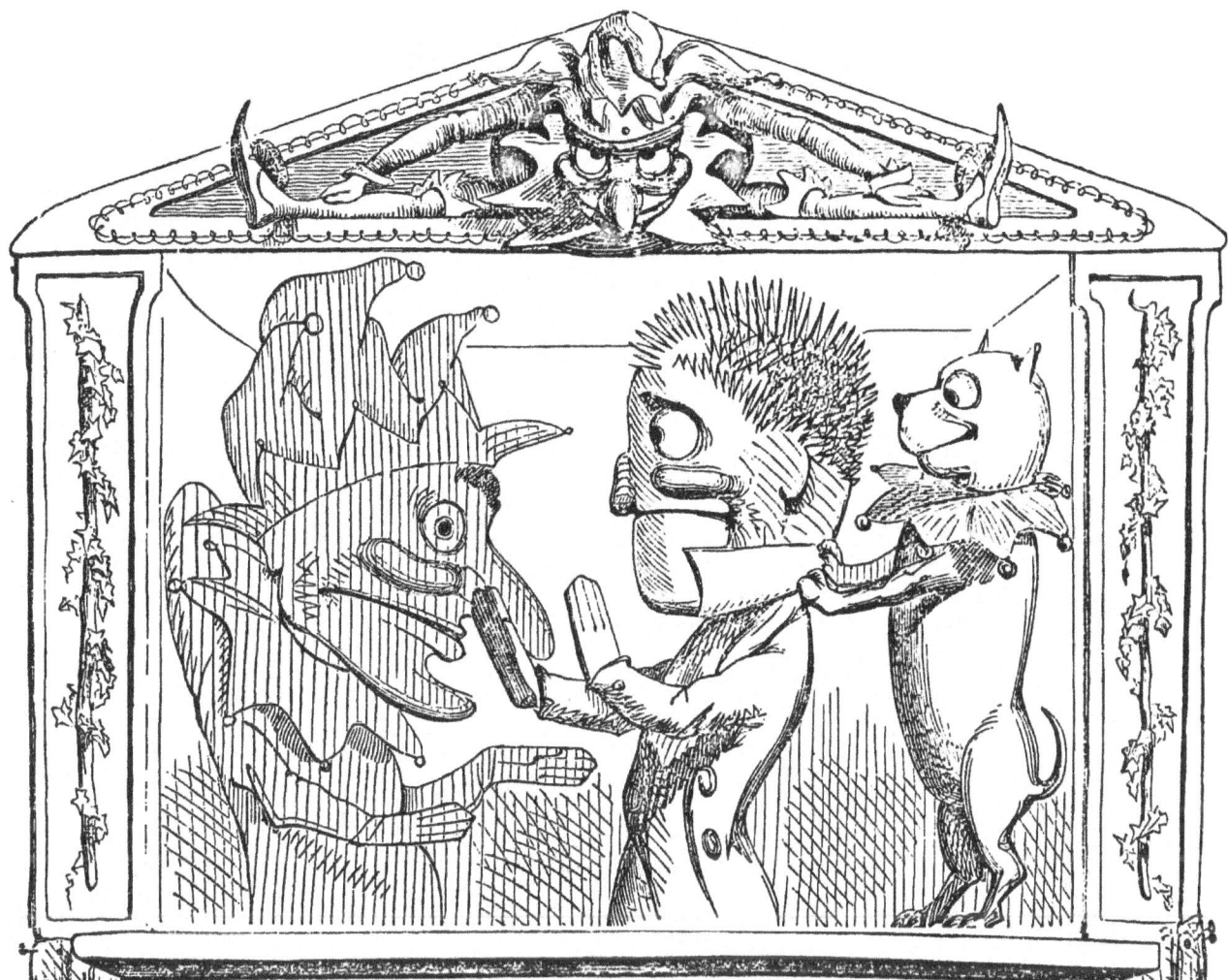

TOBY DEFENDS HIS MASTER.

Toby defends his master's right :
    It's right we should defend our masters.
I trust,—nay more, I'm certain quite,
    If *yours* should meet with like disasters
(I mean your schoolmasters), you'd do the same ;
But if you wouldn't, don't say I'm to blame.

SCENE XIX.—PUNCH, TOBY, AND JONES (*continued*).

Jones. Perhaps, Mr. Punch, you'll own he's my dog now?

Punch. No, I won't.

Jones. Then anything to please you; I'll tell you what we'll do.

Punch. What?

Jones. We'll toss up for him.

Punch. Very well.

Jones. You cry.   [*Tosses.*

Punch. Head!

Jones. Tail! It's a tail. Come along, Toby; you're mine.

Punch. He isn't! he's mine.

Jones. I cried tail.

Punch. Then take his tail! I cried head; and you shan't have that.

Jones. I'll have my half.

Punch. And I'll have mine.

> [*They pull Toby between them. The struggle lasts for some time, during which Toby sides with his former Master, by whom he is eventually carried off in triumph.*

Punch (*calling after them*). I wouldn't have him at a gift; he's got the distemper!

THE STRUGGLE FOR TOBY.

Toby has ta'en his master's part,
    With struggles fierce, and courage grim ;
That master, with ungrateful heart,
    Now wants *to take a part of him.*
Punch and the master can't contrive to hit it ;
So, to arrange their diff'rence, try to split it.

SCENE XX.—*A lapse of time is supposed to have occurred. Punch is in prison, condemned to death for his numerous crimes.*

Punch. Oh, dear! I'm in the coal-hole!

Prop. No, Mr. Punch; you are in prison!

Punch. What for?

Prop. For having broken the laws of your country.

Punch. Why, I never touched 'em.

Prop. At any rate, Mr. Punch, you will be hanged.

Punch. Hanged? Oh, dear! oh, dear!

Prop. Yes; and I hope it will be a lesson to you.

Punch. Oh, my poor wife and sixteen small children! all of 'em twins! and the oldest only two years and a half old! B-r-r-r!

　　　　　[*Weeps. The hangman rises and erects the gallows.*

Hangman. Now, Punch, you are ordered for instant execution.

Punch. What's that?

Hangman. You are to be hanged by the neck till you are dead! dead! dead!

Punch. What! three or four times over?

Hangman. No. Place your head in the centre of the rope there!

Punch (*wringing his hands*). Oh, dear! oh, dear!

PUNCH IS ORDERED FOR EXECUTION.

Punch, for his criminal career,
    At length his right to live has bartered;
He's to be hang'd.   We used to hear
    Of folks being hanged, and drawn, and quartered:
Punch can't be quartered now—that needn't awe him;
And so we've only let our artist *draw* him.

Scene XXI.—Punch and the Hangman (*continued*).

Hangman. Come, Mr. Punch ; Justice can't wait.

Punch. Stop a bit ; I haven't made my will.

Hangman. A good thought. We can't think of letting a man die till he's made his will.

Punch. Can't you ?

Hangman. Certainly not.

Punch. Then I won't make mine at all.

Hangman. That won't do, Punch. Come put your head in there.

Punch (*putting his head under the noose*). There ?

Hangman. No ; higher up !

Punch (*putting his head over*). There?

Hangman No ; lower down !

Punch. There ?

Hangman. No, you blockhead ; higher !

Punch. Well, I never was hanged before ; and I don't know how to do it.

Hangman. Oh ! as you never was hanged before, it's but right I should show you the way. Now, Mr. Punch, observe me. In the first place I put my head in the noose—so !

[*Puts his head in the noose. Punch watches attentively.*

PUNCH TAKES LESSONS IN HANGING FROM A DISTINGUISHED PROFESSOR.

Punch ne'er was hang'd before, he declares,
　　And doesn't know the way to do it;
The Hangman then the noose prepares,
　　And simply puts his own head through it,
To show him.　*I* to do so should object!
But from a hangman what can you expect?

Scene XXII.—Punch and the Hangman (*continued*).

Hangman (*with his head in the noose*). Now, Mr. Punch, you see my head?

Punch. Yes.

Hangman. Well, when I've got your head in, I pull the end of the rope.

Punch (*pulling rope a little*). So?

Hangman. Yes, only tighter.

Punch (*pulling a little more*). So?

Hangman. Tighter than that.

Punch. Very good; I think I know now.

Hangman. Then turn round and bid your friends farewell; and I'll take my head out, and you put yours in.

Punch. Stop a minute. (*Pulls the rope tightly.*) Oee! oee! oee! I understand all about it. Now, oee! oee! oee! (*Pulls the rope, and hangs the Hangman.*) Here's a man tumbled into a ditch, and hung himself up to dry.

[*Swings Hangman backwards and forwards.*

PUNCH PROFITS BY THE INSTRUCTIONS HE HAS RECEIVED, AND
HANGS THE HANGMAN.

Punch hangs the Hangman—serve him right;
   I've no compassion for the fellows
Who, 'stead of the way *from*, delight
   In showing folks that *to* the gallows.
(" Fellows" and " gallows" don't exactly rhyme,
But you shall have a better one next time.)

SCENE THE LAST.—PUNCH AND A HORRID DREADFUL PERSONAGE.

Punch (*swinging the Hangman's rope*). Oee! oee! oee!

> [*A Horrid Dreadful Personage rises behind
> Punch, and taps him on the shoulder.*

The Horrid Dreadful Personage. You're come for.

Punch (*alarmed*). Who are you?

The Horrid Dreadful Personage (*in a terrible voice*). Bogy!

Punch. Oh, dear! what do you want?

Bogy. To carry you off to the land of Bobbetty-Shooty, where you will be condemned to the punishment of shaving the monkeys.

Punch. Stop! who were you to ask for?

Bogy. Who? why, Punch, the man who was to be hanged.

Punch (*pointing to Hangman*). Then there he is!

Bogy. Oh! is that him? Thank you. Good night!

> [*Carries off Hangman.*

Punch (*knocking them both as they go*). Good night! [*Sings.*

> Root-to-to-it! Punch is right,—
> All his enemies put to flight;
> Ladies and gentlemen all, good night
>> To the freaks of Punch and Judy!   [*Exit.*

The Proprietor. Ladies hand gentlemen, the drama is concluded; and has you like it, so I hopes you'll recommend it.

> [*Bows gracefully.*

PUNCH IS VISITED BY A HORRID DREADFUL PERSONAGE.

Here's Bogy! Don't be frightened! No!
　　Laugh at him rather; and if you so
Conduct yourselves as ne'er to go
　　Astray, you'll have the right to do so.
And now I've written stanzas twenty-three;
And so good night to this fair company!

www.ingramcontent.com/pod-product-compliance
Lightning Source LLC
Chambersburg PA
CBHW081302040426
42452CB00014B/2622